OK BOOMER!

Revelations of a Baby Boomer Working with Millennials

JANET GRANGER

GET YOUR FREE COPY!
http:/JanetGranger.com/OkBoomerBook

You can get this book as a FREE download
by going to www.JanetGranger.com/OKBoomerBook

Copyright © Janet Granger, 2020. All Rights Reserved.

ISBN: 978-1-62822-008-7

Bulk discounts are available to use as promotions or for corporate training programs. For details, email janet@ janetgranger.com.

This book is also available in electronic format.
Please visit www.JanetGranger.com/OKBoomerBook for details.

BROWN SPARROW
PUBLISHING

CONTENTS

Introduction

10 Things Millennials Hate to Hear From People Over 50

10 Things People Over 50 Hate to Hear From Millennials

CONTE[NTS]

INTRODUCTION

The world is changing at a very rapid pace and, if you think of that on a timeline, right this moment, that change is the slowest it will ever be as we plunge into the future. That's an amazing reality for everyone in the workforce.

My conversation with a Millennial, Jennifer L'Heureux, helped crystallize for me why I believe the promise of this book is important. All organizations need to foster and encourage a work environment that empowers everyone - in all our glorious diversity - including various ages and generations.

Not only will we all then be able do our best – we will be happier. We'll work well with one another. And we'll help develop and grow the leaders of the next generation.

Getting along with others in our workplace - where we spend the majority of our time - can also be much more fun.

With that in mind, this book helps explain what's going on inside all of us. It helps to explain why there's friction in the workplace and why we need to fix it. Perhaps most importantly, it explains what we need to do to resolve the friction between the various generations.

How did we come to this relationship? Interaction between Baby Boomers, Gen X'ers and Millennials may have already played out in our homes. Baby Boomers are often the parents of Milennials so, as Jennifer L'Heureux points out, how Millennials think about their supervisors or managers may in some ways be informed by, or a reflection of, their relationship with their parents.

In the same way, Baby Boomers may look at Millennials, who may be the same ages as their children, with a parental authority and perspective that isn't helpful when the two generations are colleagues at work.

Gen X'ers – who often feel like the forgotten, sandwich generation, between the other two groups – can often go one way or another. They're more digitally savvy and comfortable with tech than their older counterparts, and they may also be more strategically focused than the younger generation.

If there's to be hope for a breakthrough moving forward, Gen X'ers may be in the ideal place to help, as they take over the mantle of senior leadership.

Since you've ventured this far, I encourage you to continue your journey just a little bit further. Read **10 Things Millennials Hate to Hear From People Over 50** – and **10 Things People Over 50 Hate to Hear From Millennials.** And read on to see how we can solve this situation!

10 THINGS MILLENNIALS HATE TO HEAR FROM PEOPLE OVER 50

1. When I was your age….
2. Because this is how we do it here.
3. Don't be so entitled.
4. You're too soft.
5. Why didn't you answer my email?
6. I've been doing this longer than you've been alive.
7. Get off your phone.
8. Why don't you just (advice)? It worked for me when I was your age.
9. (Mansplaining)
10. Millennials are killing the (fill in the blank) industry.

10 THINGS PEOPLE OVER 50 HATE TO HEAR FROM MILLENNIALS

1. OK, Boomer.
2. This is a waste of my time.
3. If you weren't so old, you'd realize that…
4. I don't have to listen to you – you're not my boss.
5. Unlike you, I have a life outside of work.
6. Why can't you get this (tech)?
7. Wait! I have to take a picture of this for (Insta/Snap/etc.).
8. OK, Karen.
9. You're too old to get this.
10. Why I do I need to do this? I want to make a difference.

Do any of these sound familiar?

If so, read on…

CHAPTER 1 – THE STORY OF SARAH AND THE "MILLENNIAL PROBLEM"

"I'm reaching out to you because I don't know what else to do," Sarah writes, in an email. "I see that you've written and talked about Baby Boomers. Can we talk about this to see if it's something you can help with?"

I respond to Sarah and ask to set up a call, to hear more details about her situation.

"I can't do my job," she confides, when we talk, "and my boss is a Baby Boomer. He just doesn't understand me or what I'm trying to do here. I'm in charge of the social media team, globally," she continues, "and I just can't do my job anymore. I've tried everything and nothing has worked. So I'm hoping maybe you can help."

My heart goes out to Sarah. This isn't the first time I've heard someone in her position talk about this issue, and it won't be the last.

Sarah's situation is of particular interest to me because it's the first time that I've had a Millennial reach out to me to help her with her relationship to Baby Boomers – her boss and his boss, as it turns out, as well as the rest of senior management in the organization. In most cases, I hear from Baby Boomers who want to talk about the Millennials they work with who are "so hard to deal with."

Sarah sounds so unhappy and depressed; I ask if it's possible to meet. I've met many hard-working marketing managers like her and I can feel her sense of urgency.

We make an appointment to have lunch outside her office building, which is key in these situations because it gets Sarah out of the office. We pick a place far away from her building so she doesn't worry about who may be there or over-hearing our conversation.

"I'm in charge of the marketing and social media team globally," she shares, "and we can't get any funding for our campaigns. Management expects us to do marketing, but we can't even get a budget approved. My team has lost faith in me. If I can't get any funds for our campaigns, they can't do much of anything."

Though she is calm and professional, I can see Sarah is starting to feel desperate. She won't say it, yet, but she's wondering if she belongs in her position and in the organization itself.

She's young to be in such a position of management and responsibility but I can see that she deserves it. As we talk, it's clear that she knows a great deal about her job (digital marketing) and she is a good leader for her teams, located throughout the U.S.

Sarah is professional in her approach to me and to the situation. She describes the various ways she's thought of and tried to get budget for the work she and her team need to do. Digital marketing is fast becoming a "play to pay" world, and it's starting to get harder to break through the clutter with "free" methods, such as organic social media (Facebook, Instagram, etc.).

In addition, there are other costs associated with digital marketing for a large organization, from subscription to technical platforms, to creating beautiful and valuable images, to generating written "content." Digital marketing is a fast-paced field and it's critical to stay up-to-date when working on the front lines, creating and executing marketing campaigns.

Sarah is not alone

Do you have someone like Sarah working in your organization? Do you recognize the signs of younger people struggling in their roles – either as an individual contributor or as a manager with a team? Here are some of the signs to look for and recognize:

- Lack of involvement or engagement at work (one example is someone who is a loner, doesn't interact with anyone, and doesn't make eye contact during meetings)
- Teams that struggle to reach their goals
- Emails and other correspondence that's not returned or responded to in a timely way – or at all
- Lack of meeting attendance
- Meetings that have long silences when no one will speak up
- "Bickering" within a group or team
- Hostile emails or personal interactions among colleagues or peers

These are classic signs that there's a problem brewing, one that no one is addressing. Have you seen any of these in your organization? Or on one of your teams? Or is this you, too?

Here's a quick exercise

If you find you're nodding your head in agreement to any of this, take a moment to sit back. Put this book down (or stop reading online), and think about what you've seen in your organization and what you may be experiencing, yourself.

Reread the list above and, focusing on each bullet point. Think of all the instances where you've seen this happen – either with other people, or even recalling your own actions.

I'd like you to make a list – write it down or type it out – of all the people you've seen this happen to. Or how you've been feeling, if you're the one caught in this dilemma. Just write it out, as if you're talking back to me.

You can stop reading here to do this and pick up at the next paragraph after you've finished.

Thanks!

If you've witnessed this in your organization or even in your own feelings and behavior – I have a name for this. I call it the generational divide. As a marketer, I recognized this years ago, working with my older colleagues (all Baby Boomers) when they were confronted with the changes taking place in marketing.

What created this new generational divide?

I've been throwing out terms like Millennials and Baby Boomers, so it's time I define these properly. These generational terms are for people born within a certain timeframe. Here's the generally recognized generation that comprises each group:

- Baby Boomers – born from 1945 – 1964
- Gen X'ers – born from 1965 – 1981
- Gen Y/Millennials – born from 1981 – 1994
- Gen Z – born after 1995

Now that the terms are clear, let's use these timeframes as background to understand how we got here. I'm going to look back at the past 30 years or so of marketing – when the paradigm shifted from what's now called "outbound" marketing to "inbound" marketing (online).

Back in the early 1990s, when I started in marketing - along with my Baby Boomer colleagues - there wasn't yet an internet. I know it's hard to imagine now, but before the internet existed there were still many ways to reach both consumers and businesses. The mail was used much more widely, for example, so there were mailers that were written, designed, and printed, then sent out to via the U.S. Postal Service.

In addition, there were print ads everywhere: in magazines (which people read all the time), newspapers (local and national, as well as international), and other areas, such as "food coupons" in the Sunday section of newspapers.

Other popular channels for marketing were radio, television, and the newest kid on the block: cable television. Cable systems around the U.S. were set up and figured out, early on, how to sell advertising - both nationally and locally. This created a boom in both new networks that evolved, to serve more and more niche markets. In addition, it gave local businesses a way to reach people, inexpensively, who lived in the areas they were located.

Then, in the 1990s, the internet was invented. As with all new technologies, there were those who jumped aboard right away, those who watched to see what would happen, and those who ignored it entirely, sticking their heads in the sand and hoping it would go away so they wouldn't have to deal with it.

I've written a book about these three types of workers: "Digital Influence for Baby Boomers: Why You Should Care and Yes, You Can Do This." How marketing Boomers reacted to the invention of the internet had a profound effect on the rest of their careers.

The early internet

For those who jumped onto the internet early, in the 1990s, working at places such as Dow Jones and using the internet for their work, it was clear that they were able to do much more than their colleagues, who were still working "the old way." The information available to them gave them a leg up on their competition and soon many in the financial world were moving online in order to get the most current information and to share information quickly.

Marketing shifted, also. The web inspired more and more start-ups, creating the beginning of what is now, for Baby Boomers, remembered as the Dot Com era, named for the many new websites springing up daily, named with .com URLs.

That led to a financing frenzy for those early internet companies that had lots of users but, perhaps, no source of revenues or financial model to turn a profit. Marketing online at that time was typically e-commerce – using websites allowed brick-and-mortar stores to expand past their catalogs to sell products.

This was the environment that spawned Amazon, which began selling books online and soon expanded to peddling other products. It also spawned Google, which recognized early on that people were searching for various goods - and information - online.

In a few years, this blossoming of new websites led to the Dot Com "bust." Many websites that -initially - had been highly valued, gathering lots of investment dollars, proved to be nothing but big black holes of expenses, with little (or no) stream of revenues.

In 2002, this reality-shattering phenomenon burst the bubble in the financial market, creating a recession - though that downturn now seems almost inconsequential, compared to the market crash of 2008 and with the recent COVID-19 crash.

How marketing evolved

Savvy marketers held fast to the online model, however, and weathered this time and the following growth of online marketing. As Google's dominance grew, as well as other newcomers, such as social media, it became clear that the internet was a new channel to be explored and mined to capture the attention and spending power of consumers and businesses.

Early adaptors to this market were nonprofits, always on the lookout to find new ways to generate revenues from donors and members. In addition to the retailers, who'd moved their catalogs online, others began to take advantage of the low-cost of entry to market online. Websites were created quickly and styles of design were adapted to make them more attractive. Platforms were designed to make it easier to buy online.

With the rapid growth of social media came new ways to market – Facebook being the first. Though it's used now by the older generation, Facebook started off being the best place to market to college students and younger buyers. Facebook also recognized when a new upstart, Instagram, started to take Facebook's place, rising quickly in acceptance and use. So Facebook purchased Instagram.

Nowadays, these two channels reach very different markets. Facebook is predominantly used by people over the age of 40, while Instagram is the favorite of those who are younger. And then there's Snapchat and TikTok, used by even younger generations, down to teens and adolescents.

These are very broad generalizations so I suspect that you, as a reader, can think of others (perhaps yourself?) who fall outside these general parameters. Please note that I use these age groups and demarcations only to outline what I've seen and experienced as a digital marketer, working with a wide variety of small, medium, and enterprise businesses over the years.

The reality of digital marketing is that it's moving and changing by the week, if not by the day. So many new technologies exist now that didn't five years ago. There's the ability to add live chat to websites, for example - or chat bots that are programmed with pre-written scripts and answers.

On social media, it seems to change daily. There's every permutation of live video: Facebook Live, Instagram Live, as well as YouTube Live. There are all sorts of fun filters on Instagram and Snapchat. There are Instagram Stories. Plus TikTok, which roared into existence and popularity within a matter of months, not years.

The way the world is changing has approached breakneck speed

Here's a chart, to provide a sense of the speed with which people are now adapting to new technologies, compared to how long it took for new technologies to "take hold" in the public in years past.

Technology adoption in US households, 1903 to 2019

Technology adoption rates, measured as the percentage of households in the United States using a particular technology.

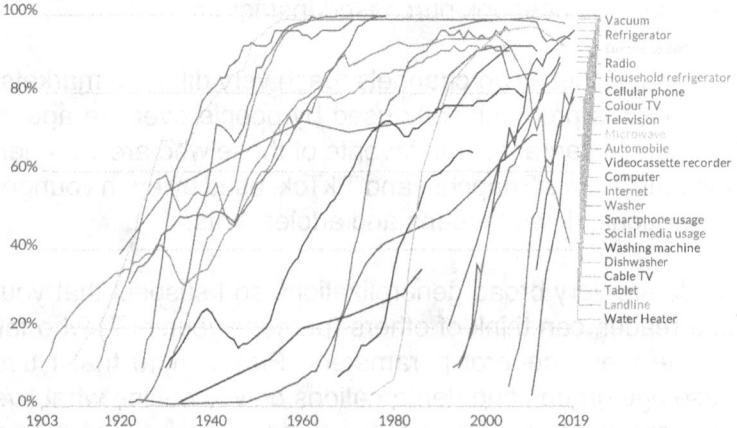

Vacuum
Refrigerator

Radio
Household refrigerator
Cellular phone
Colour TV
Television
Microwave
Automobile
Videocassette recorder
Computer
Internet
Washer
Smartphone usage
Social media usage
Washing machine
Dishwasher
Cable TV
Tablet
Landline
Water Heater

Source: Comin and Hobijn (2004) and others   OurWorldinData.org/technology-adoption/ • CC BY
Note: See the sources tab for definitions of household adoption, or adoption rates, by technology type.

This is an important element in Sarah's story because it points to the way people, in the past, have taken more time to recognize, try, and then change their behaviors to do things differently, based on the invention, cost, and availability of new technologies.

Think about Baby Boomers, who were born from 1945 - 1964. Looking at the purple line, for example, which represents dishwashers (a luxury for many), starts in 1920 and doesn't go higher than a 1% adoption rate until the early 1960s, when it rises to 9% usage (in the U.S.), 32% usage in 1972, and 62% in the early 2000's.

Much faster adoption in a Baby Boomer's lifetime is cable television, which started at 7% in the 1960s and rose to over 60% usage in 30 years. Faster than that is the convenience of microwave ovens, which were invented and commercialized in the early 1970s and zoomed to over 82% in only 20 years. Then there's the everyday computer, which was in 21% of U.S. households in 1995 and rose to 63% by 2003, only eight years later.

Compare that to what's happened in the lifetimes of Millennials, born from 1981 – 1996. As children in the 1980s and '90s and teenagers in the '90s through the mid-2000s, they witnessed cell phones and the internet, both at about 10% usage in 1994, rocket up to 34% - or roughly one-third of everyone they know (depending on where they lived) having internet and a cell phone in 1999, only five years later.

Five years after that, roughly half of the population had internet (57%) and 63% had cell phones, in 2004. And by 2011, the majority of people in the U.S. had internet (76%) and cell phones (89%). Within the relatively short span of their lives, the world went wireless and was doing business online.

That rapid speed of technology development and its adoption has led many older people to remark: "Millennials were born with cell phones in their hands." Indeed, all this technology was adopted at the same time that this generation came of age.

Change – in technology and otherwise – causes fear

This rapid speed of change in technology affected everyone, not only socially (as social media blossomed) but at work. How the U.S. conducts business now - versus how it was done in the 1990s and even in the early 2000s - is radically different.

Here are five examples of how organizations ran up through the 1900s:

1) A great deal of office work could only be done at the business location because there was no internet to connect everyone, everywhere.

2) Paperwork has declined significantly at work. Many Millennials may not know what an "inbox" referred to. (When paper worked its way through organizations, there was so much of it that each person had an "inbox" to receive new paperwork.)

3) When people left their offices, or places of work, they were inaccessible, even in their cars. There were no cell phones – only land lines. When employees were out of their home or their office, they were unreachable.

If they were in a profession where they had to be reached, no matter where they were (such as doctors, for instance), they wore beepers. These vibrated, sometimes showing the number of the person calling, so they could call back or go where they were needed.

4) One of the biggest status symbols at the office was having an enclosed room/office. In many cases, younger employees started off at a desk - in more team-like settings. As they got promoted, they moved to more and more private spaces. The big "coup" was getting the "corner office," with beautiful views out of two big windows.

5) Through the 1990s, direct mail was a viable way to send out advertising messages. Very few people now think of mail as a way to send advertising (yet, curiously, there is so little mail now that it's a good way to avoid the clutter of online communications!).

All of these changes in how we work put people who've become accustomed to something else in an uncomfortable position. They are literally out of their comfort zone, having to learn new ways to do things. How to move from paper to online. How to "be on call" all the time - via their cell phones. How to deal with working, physically, in different types of spaces – not having that coveted office, or privacy - although that may change drastically after COVID-19.

Add to that, dealing with people working all around them all day, wearing headphones or ear buds. Communicating a different way – online vs. on the phone or in person.

If there's one universal fear that everyone shares it is the fear of change. Everyone who learned how to work one way is fearful about having to change all that. Fearful of having to learn 'how' to work all over again. Fearful of the people who seem to do this easily, and fearful of how easily they can do it, as opposed to how hard it is to change.

Getting back to the point of this history lesson – the intergenerational divide

The reason for this brief history lesson was to help us all

understand how we got to what I've called **the digital divide**, or perhaps more appropriately outside the marketing industry, the **intergenerational divide.**

All of this was to explain how, looking back at the past 30 years or so, the paradigm has shifted for older workers, who learned how to be productive in a world that, frankly, no longer exists. And how that affects working with younger people who don't seem to have much difficulty at all, in this new work environment.

So let's talk about Sarah's generation and the "new normal" of Millennials dominating in the workplace.

CHAPTER 2 – THE NEW NORMAL – MILLENNIALS IN THE WORKPLACE

The story of Sarah is not unusual, and yet it feels like a new phenomenon.

Why? Because Sarah is now part of the dominant story in the U.S. workforce.

To make sure everyone understands the terms I'm using, here's a recap of the definitions and "nicknames" for different generation segments since WWII:

- Baby Boomers – born from 1945 – 1964 (after the end of WWII)
- Gen X'ers – born from 1965 – 1981
- Gen Y/Millennials – born from 1981 – 1994
- Gen Z – born in 1995 and later

If you think about it, the ages of people in the U.S. workforce has always been in flux. There are always older generations and younger generations. However, each generation is slightly different in size.

For example, the "Baby Boom" was called that because of the unprecedented "boom" of births that happened after WWII, when the soldiers came home, and there were government-created incentives and programs (in what was referred to as the "GI bill") enabling them to go to college, buy homes, and start families.

Baby Boomers started entering the labor force in the 1960s and having children of their own. In fact, those at the very end of the Baby Boom were having children in the 1980s and 1990s. These are the Gen Y, now called Millennials, who entered the labor force starting in the 1990s.

With that in mind, here's an interesting graph from the Pew Research Center that shows the composition of the U.S. labor force, by generation, from 1994 to 2017.

Millennials became the largest generation in the labor force in 2016

U.S. labor force, in millions

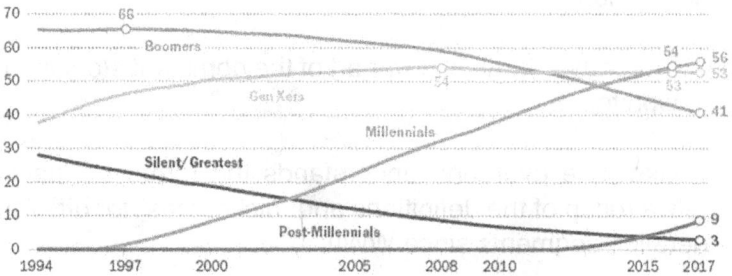

Note: Labor force includes those ages 16 and older who are working or looking for work. Annual averages shown.
Source: Pew Research Center analysis of monthly 1994-2017 Current Population Survey (IPUMS).
PEW RESEARCH CENTER

As you can see, back in the 1990s, Baby Boomers made up about 66% of the U.S. labor force. This is why I referenced the 1990s in the previous chapter, to show how "business got done" by a majority of Baby Boomers. If you look at the chart back in 1994, almost 30% of the labor force was the Silent/ Greatest generation, referring to the parents of the Boomers.

Millennials started to enter the job market in the late 1990s and have been playing a larger and larger role throughout the early 2000s to the present day. The "tipping point" - where Millennials outnumbered Baby Boomers - was in 2013. You can see where the lines cross in the previous above. This data ends in 2017, as Millennials became the largest sector of the U.S. labor force.

So you might ask, at this point, **if Millennials are the dominant generation working, why are there such issues?**

The answer lies with **who makes up senior management**

in most organizations. While Baby Boomers represent less than 40% of the labor force, their seniority means that, in many cases, they are the owners, CEOs, Presidents and senior partners, along with filling other senior management roles in many organizations. They are the ones formulating the strategy and holding the budget purse strings in many mid-size to larger organizations (with notable exceptions in new technology companies).

If it's not Baby Boomers in these roles, it's often older Gen X'ers - people over the age of 40, for example. Gen X'ers are an interesting group because the oldest were born in the late 1960s and early 1970s and comprised about 50% of the workforce in the late 1990s. Like Baby Boomers, many Gen X'ers worked "the old-fashioned way" early in their careers.

Remember the examples I gave?

They started in offices, where it was important what time you got there and what time you left. They coveted the prestige of the "corner office." They may have been young enough to adopt new tech more easily since they came of age as the office environment was using desktop computers and the internet played an increasingly larger role.

So, in some ways, they are less fearful when it comes to new technology. But they are in an interesting space in between Boomers and Millennials because they have a foot in both camps.

This means that, as senior managers now, they may act like Baby Boomers while being young enough to relate to older Millennials, who are in their late 30's. For this reason, they are often referred to as the "in between" generation.

Gen Z is close behind

But wait, there's more!

This intergenerational clash in the workplace doesn't just end with Boomers, Gen X'ers, and Millennials. Gen Z is entering the workforce, too. If you look at the graph, this "Post Millennials" group is coming of age now - with the oldest born in 1995 - which makes them the youngest in the workplace (25 years old, as of 2020). By 2017, they comprised 10% of the labor force, and this number will continue to grow.

Generation Z came of age as the world became digital. They are totally comfortable with technology, as well as the rapid technological change that intimidates many older workers. They can't remember when phones weren't mobile; as teenagers, they had cell phones.

Were you aware of the "Ok Boomer" dismissive statement, which implied "you're just old - be that way - and I'll ignore you?" With this type of attitude - not among all of them, but certainly part of the cultural experience - it's no wonder that Baby Boomers bristle at their criticism. Boomers themselves grew up in the 1960s and 1970s - an era of cultural revolt - so to be dismissed by the younger generation feels both ironic and hurtful.

This is not to say that the resentment and dismissiveness that many younger people, especially teenagers, feel about older generations has no merit.

Within the past 30 years, the economic disparity of poor versus wealthy in the U.S. has grown wider and wider. And the issue of global warming has been either ignored or pushed aside by many older leaders.

Greta Thunburg's stunning rise to prominence as a student activist and the voice of many in her generation illustrates the betrayal and dismay many of her generation feel about how their predecessors - Baby Boomers, in particular - have handled power and leadership.

What does this all mean?

The significance of Gen Z comprising 10% of the labor force (and growing), as well as Millennials comprising close to 60% of the labor force, means that, right now, Baby Boomers and older Gen X'ers are clearly outnumbered. While they may still be the ones "in power" as senior managers, they find themselves in an increasingly smaller and smaller circles of like-minded people.

This has led to the current crisis in the workplace. So let's talk about the workplace a little bit more to understand why there's a problem.

Working together

We've just covered why there's a new "crisis" in the workplace, as Baby Boomers and Gen X'ers are now outnumbered by Millennials, combined with Gen Z, who comprise 65% of the U.S. labor force.

Why is this an issue now?

Some research into the scholarship behind the concept of teamwork reveals that an organization's success depends, to a great extent, on the ability of people to work well together.

> *Contemporary firms consider teamwork as an essential feature of a successful business…. Organizations that are focused on developing teamwork are likely to experience numerous benefits including better and improved decision making, flexibility amongst workforce and focus on achieving organizational goals with highly motivated workforce and synergy among team members.* *

Most managers and leaders recognize this, which is why many focus their attention on hiring, team-building, and teamwork.

But the idea of teamwork varies, depending on the person you are talking to. It's important to understand the differences in how each generation approaches the idea of "teamwork."

Here are some examples.

Teamwork – what it means for Baby Boomers

Baby Boomers were the first generation "to ever be graded on a report card 'works well/plays well with others.'"

Learning how to cooperate as a child led to an ongoing expectation that people will work well together. So around the 1980s, when these Boomers grew up and started managing people, they focused on developing teams in the office. This was when activities were created to build teams, strengthen teams, and hold team meetings.

Teamwork also meant that people did what was expected of them - fulfilling their roles dutifully. They were encouraged to put in the work, as requested by management and leaders.

When Baby Boomers began their careers, they were usually assigned the "grunt" work in many offices. This included low-skilled tasks like copying documents, printing and collating documents, etc. The goal was to "learn the business" by watching, observing, being a part of it but not in control (yet).

Because they were raised to be "team players," they did these tasks without a lot of complaints. That's what was expected of them. Indeed, the organizational culture fostered an expectation that "everyone started out at the bottom" and "had to pay their dues."

As Baby Boomers moved up the ranks in organizations - in the 1980s and 1990s - they expected the same behavior (and attitude) among those they hired to do the same type of work. Gen X'ers came into these types of cultures and did the same as the Boomers – paying their dues, working hard, and moving ahead.

However - during the 1990s - the internet and software programs were invented. These new tools helped alleviate the more menial work tasks. Think of document and spreadsheet software, which allowed for easier rewrites, editing, calculating, etc., as well as online document writing and editing programs, which helped to make edits and rewrites as easy as "retyping."

All these software advances took the burden of menial tasks away from junior employees (or, in some instances, secretaries and administrative assistants, which is how many women first entered the workplace).

Teamwork – what it means for Millennials

Millennials are just as interested in the idea of teamwork as Baby Boomers - even more, it can be said. But the way they think about the concept 'teamwork' is quite different. Recent research indicates that Millennials love working in teams when it means they can learn from others in a collaborative experience and be part of projects that are inclusive (i.e. not done in functional silos).

They also appreciate working in teams or in organizations that are on the forefront of their field or industry so they can feel they are part something bigger and important. In particular, they like being a part of a company or group that is innovative, new, fast-paced, or disruptive.

Many Millennials watched their parents (or their friends' parents) lose their jobs during the early 2000s or the Great Recession in 2008. They saw how the Boomer generation was loyal to - and worked long hours for - companies that didn't appreciate them when times got tough.

In response, Millennials look at companies from a much less loyal, more dispassionate perspective. For them, it has to be a mutually beneficial arrangement or they're not interested in being part of the team or staying around.

This more "people-centered" approach means that - if Millennials feel appreciated and well treated - they'll stay and work hard. But if they're not treated well, they won't stick around. While they long for the stability of an established organization (having lived through uncertain times in their younger years), they want to feel they are vital and contributing in their roles at all times.

So, going back to an earlier example, when it comes to doing menial work, "entry level" tasks, Millennials not only balk about having to do this type of work - they also make it clear that they are not interested in the idea of "paying their dues." They expect to have more responsibility when they start to work, considering this the way they "create an impact" with their efforts.

One great outcome has been avoiding more menial tasks, Millennials are creative and innovative about coming up with alternatives. In many cases, they turn to technology to do the work, instead. Or they work collaboratively to discover alternatives to anyone having to do the repetitive, boring work, or find ways to reduce it.

Often times, Millennials may have ideas or technology options that haven't been explored. They can then team with senior members, who have the knowledge and expertise, to figure out how to make new processes work.

There's work to be done here

With the differences in how the different generations perceive and approach teamwork, it's no wonder that many teams are "missing the mark" when it comes to good working relationships and generating results.

As one Human Resource specialist has noted: "It always amazes me that we are still discussing how to bridge the generational divide in organizations. When I started... 15 years ago, I never imaged the issue of how to motivate, engage, and collaborate across different generations would be relevant for this long."

Aside from teamwork, what are some other Human Resource issues that are hurting organizational performance and results? Here are just a few:

- Millennials are the "least engaged" generation in the workforce at present, with 55% responding in a poll that they are not engaged.
- According to the HR specialist company Robert Half, 28% of new hires (most of them Millennials) leave their positions within the first 90 days. Why is that?
- 25% of Millennials have quit a job because of a Boomer colleague.

It's clear there are issues - right now - dividing teams that need to be addressed. The question is, why hasn't this been done yet? Has this worked in the past? Let's take a look at what's new and different now, between the generations, and what's actually been around for a while. This can help us best determine the way forward.

CHAPTER 3 – WORKING TOGETHER

We've just touched on the broader issues that are now apparent between the older generations (Boomers and Gen X'ers over 45 or 50 years old) and Millennials, who now comprise the majority of the workforce (with Gen Z'ers close behind).

Let's take a holistic look at the workplace and delve into how we got here - to see what inter-generational challenges we've had in the past in the U.S. and how we've dealt with them successfully. This can provide insights as we move forward. Plus, we can look at what's different now than in the past. This perspective can help us to forge different, innovative paths forward.

Challenges we've always had

If you think about the history of the workforce - from year to year, decade to decade - it's clear that there has always been a mixture of age groups working together.

Baby Boomers came into the workforce starting in the mid-to-late 1960s. At that time, their managers and supervisors were the "Silent Generation," born in an era that included the Great Depression (1929). This older generation grew up at a time when there was so much poverty in the U.S., they learned to cherish everything and save everything they could.

I remember my father saving every nail he took out of a board - or found - "just in case" he needed it at some point in the future. I've also heard stories about mothers taking jars that had jelly in them and, instead of throwing them out when they were empty, filling them up halfway with milk, closing and shaking them, to create a "delicious milkshake." Nothing went to waste!

When this generation worked with Baby Boomers, they also felt an immense divide and "culture clash." This young, upstart Boomer generation had never experienced real hardship, growing up in an increasingly prosperous climate and economic era in the U.S. These Baby Boomers were perceived as "spoiled" and soft, because they hadn't been challenged by deprivation or hardship.

Is any of this starting to sound familiar?

If you think about the nature of work - especially in an office environment - there have always been older workers and younger workers. The older generation doesn't understand the younger generation, and the younger generation is constantly pushing the older generation to try new methods, think differently, and not be afraid of change. This is the reality of the "human condition" and we're not going to be able to change that!

And it goes further. Consider this: employees of the same generation tend to feel most comfortable with others who are like them - of the same general age. They may have lunch together, get coffee, and socialize at work and, perhaps, get together outside of work.

There's nothing wrong with this, of course. Each parallel generation is doing the same thing. It's natural that the generations may choose to segregate themselves by age. Yet - in general - though not in all cases, this can be counter-productive when it comes to team-building.

Why are teams important?

Let's talk about the nature of teams for a moment. What is the point of having a team at all? What's the goal? And are they really so important?

Team building is about generating a sense of trust and cooperation among the members of a group of people. The goal is to create a sense of belonging and familiarity so that each team member feels a connection and can see how they are part of a larger group.

As one Human Resources company describes it, "A team is a group of people organized to work together interdependently and cooperatively to meet the needs of their customers by accomplishing their purpose and goals." These "customers" can be other internal groups or employees, as well as outside customers or clients.

The best teams at work

The best teams at work those who trust and respect one another (please note: they don't necessarily have to be friends - as long as there is trust and respect). The best team members are those who put aside their differences to focus on the goal(s) they are trying to accomplish. The better a group of people can do this as a team, the better the results of the work itself.

Getting back to our example earlier, if members of a team are only building work relationships with people who are "just like them" in age, then they're subtly building competitive teams against those who differ from them. This can cause those who are not part of the group to feel different, excluded, and see themselves as outsiders, rather than feeling that they belong.

In summary: If members of your team are only building relationships with those from their generation, this can harm overall productivity in the workplace. It also impacts innovation and creativity by limiting the diversity of thought - and not engaging or communicating with others who may have a different point of view.

The importance of team diversity

There are many reasons diversity is important – but the most compelling one for business owners and managers is that *diverse teams actually perform better!*

This was verified by a McKinsey study, summarized in the Harvard Business Review, that examined the financial results of organizations that had more diverse managers, where diversity was defined by ethnic, racial, and gender differences.

> *A 2015 McKinsey report on 366 public companies found that those in the top quartile for ethnic and racial diversity in management were 35% more likely to have financial returns above their industry mean, and those in the top quartile for gender diversity were 15% more likely to have returns above the industry mean.*

I'm a big fan of data and the power of what data tells us. This data tells me that - not only is it a better idea to have a diverse employment pool based on the population – it also makes business sense to strive for diversity in the workplace.

So it's best to **look at workplace diversity as a business goal and strategy for success.** This means hiring for diversity, retaining your employees to keep diversity, and taking advantage of that mixture in your workplace.

Taking advantage of diversity means celebrating and focusing on that mixture, being intentional about it, and ensuring that everyone is conscious of and respectful of it.

This may seem counter-intuitive for those who approach diversity as an "unspoken" - even taboo - issue. Please note:

this focus on diversity isn't about focusing on differences, or on discrimination based on differences. It's about celebrating diversity and being conscious of and intentional about making people with diverse backgrounds feel they are critical to success.

With the issue of age diversity, I believe that the differences should be celebrated so that each generation can help others with their talents and their different perspective.

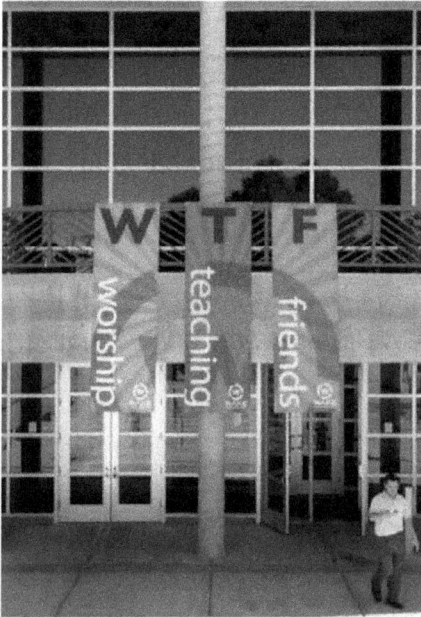

How a lack of diversity can be a disadvantage, too

Looked at it in reverse, a lack of diversity can lead to unintended consequences, such as tone- deaf messaging or a communication that misses the mark entirely.

Look at these church banners that were created and displayed for all to see. Notice anything provocative about it?

It's a lovely idea - the concept of church representing Worship, Teaching and Friend. But there's a fundamental problem with this display. To Millennials, the acronym spelled out at the top, as each banner has the letters boldly outlined, is WTF. To them, this popular acronym, reads "what the f**k?"

If the person or group that came up with these banners had a Millennial involved in the process, they would surely have avoided this mistake. To me, this says that whoever created this display was an older group that didn't acknowledge or reach out to younger people - perhaps those they were trying to attract - to ask them how the banners resonated with them!

This example illustrates why having multi-generational representation in any working group is absolutely critical. This is especially true if the goal is to understand what younger colleagues want and what they feel is important.

In strict marketing terms, if you're trying to communicate to someone, it's important to know what messages resonate with them and what is important to them, too.

Mistakes like these are not new. There have been classic gaffs for each generation. For example, the Anti-Drug PSA campaign aimed at youth in the 1980s, telling them to "just say no" to drugs, actually increased drug use at the time. (Talk about backfiring...)

Another of the great gaffs in the 1980s, for example, was a Calvin Klein ad campaign for underwear that bordered on child pornography. They were trying to appeal to a younger audience, and it was a total failure of taste and meaning.

Now that we've talked about why teamwork and team diversity is so important to organizational success, we can turn our focus back on what's different now that's different from work diversity in the past, especially with regard to age and generational differences.

To put it another way: if there have always been different age groups working together, why is this such a pain point now? What makes this current generational gap so important?

Talented, valuable people are leaving organizations because of the generational divide

What makes this issue so imperative now is that it's driving people to leave organizations. Here's some interesting data from a survey done in 2020 to Millennials and Baby Boomers who self-reported as working full-time in a variety of industries - split about 50/50 between male and female respondents.

The survey found that 33% of Millennials and 39% of Baby Boomers indicated they would leave their current job within the next six months. Granted - this may have changed dramatically with the COVID-19 experience that hit the U.S. full force in March 2020.

The reason why they want to leave - which is most telling - is this: 30% of Millennials who responded said they feel they're being held back "by an older colleague" and 25% have actually quit jobs because of an older boss, manager, or colleague. That means one out of every four Millennials who has quit their job did it because of an older worker.

The influence of this generational gap gets worse, unfortunately. According to Baby Boomer respondents, 36% have quit their jobs because of a Millennial boss, manager or colleague! And 52% report they've experienced age discrimination at work.

Those are pretty stunning figures when it comes to the prevalence of unhappiness at work. This may change somewhat as unemployment becomes a worse issue than unhappiness and if there are fewer choice options. People who need their paychecks to survive are more likely to tough it out in a difficult situation.

However, a 2018 Harvard Business Review study indicated that it's not just the people/personality aspect at play. It's also the nature of the work - as defined by the supervisor, boss, or manager. According to this study, younger workers are leaving jobs that don't take advantage of all of their talents.

Their conclusion is that "it's up to managers to design jobs that are too good to leave."

Whatever the case - the boss him/herself or the job limitations that a manager creates - it's clear that the value of our human resources is not being taken seriously enough in the workplace. And the revolving door of people leaving (when circumstances permit) illustrates the crisis of conflict that is occurring at the team level.

In addition, there are other inter-generational challenges that are caused by the advances made by technology over the past 30 years.

The digital divide

I've been calling the difference between older and younger workers the digital divide since I started seeing it played out in various marketing departments and agencies as early as 2010.

From my perspective, it was clear that the advances of internet technology and online sophistication had changed the focus from what was called "outbound" marketing to "inbound" marketing.

To stay relevant, and to have the company I worked for stay relevant, I learned about the power of this new digital channel, hired agencies to teach me about all the new digital options, and shifted our marketing efforts and campaigns in this new direction.

Not everyone in my department - or the company - made that same shift, so the ones who did stood out. One younger colleague, my counter-part in a different division, was about six months ahead of me in making in this shift; he ended up leaving the company to go to Facebook.

This seemed to be the trend: agencies that I hired, and internal employees who happened to be younger (such as Gen X'ers and Millennials), were doing the same thing I was doing, making the seismic shift online; they supported my efforts and I supported theirs. But many older colleagues did not; they "didn't understand" the new platforms and, because of that, avoided them.

As time progressed and digital marketing catapulted ahead, gaining in influence, reach, as well as complexity and sophistication, more and more of my older colleagues plunged their heads into the sand, like ostriches, trying to ignore or avoid the change that was happening all around them. Soon, phrases like "digital transformation" surrounded them and, terrified, they shut their eyes, pulling deeper and deeper into themselves, away from the change enveloping them.

When you ignore the shifting sands of change, they bury you. I witnessed this time and time again. So who survives in a changing and shifting world? Those who keep up, ride the new wave, and dig deep into the new reality. It was the younger employees and agencies, who saw and anticipated the shifts: moving into social media, for example, or focusing on search engine optimization and pay-per-click, who were at the forefront of marketing.

These younger marketers were comfortable with the new technologies. The younger they were, in fact, the more facile they were in adapting and taking advantage of the new applications popping up constantly, and in navigating the intricacies of each emerging digital technology. I came to work with them, more and more, and to rely on them to keep up with the rapid pace of change and marketing opportunity.

It became clear that, because of their comfort and ease with learning these new technologies, there was a digital divide between the generations. The Millennials kept pace and enjoyed it; the Baby Boomers - many of whom were my colleagues and above me in senior management - shut their eyes in confusion and let the younger generations run with it.

Where we are now

And that's how we got to this place in time, where there's a digital divide in the workplace. There have always been differences in the generations; this time, the rapid pace of technology change and growth has left older workers behind. What happened in marketing – the shift towards digital – has happened in other functional areas and industries across the board.

Now, we're seeing technology emerge as its own powerhouse. The leaders in tech: Google, Apple, Facebook, and others have created an industry where none existed before. Because of them, and other tech (such as smartphones), other industries are now ruled by the advance of technology - leaving older workers behind.

Think about the change in wealth management, for example. Baby Boomers are accustomed to inter-personal relationships with their clients and "hand-holding" over the phone. Younger workers in this sector need to understand what Boomers are looking for; at the same time, they understand (perhaps more intuitively) what younger investors seek and need, with regard to digital communications and touch points.
Let's consider this now in the greater context of Sarah's predicament - what's different in the workplace now - and what's constant.

CHAPTER 4: WHAT'S DIFFERENT NOW – AND WHAT'S NOT

What about Sarah? To recap quickly, Sarah reached out to me because she didn't know what else to do. She couldn't do her job, managing a digital marketing team at an international nonprofit, and she knew I have experience working with Baby Boomers in digital marketing.

As she suspected, her boss didn't understand what her team was trying to do or why they needed the budget they requested. When I spoke with him, he was frustrated, too.

"We can post on Facebook and Instagram for free," he told me, "I can do that myself. Why do they need this budget?"

It was clear to me that Sarah's boss, and the rest of senior management - didn't understand much about digital marketing. As Sarah had told me, while they expected her team to "do marketing," they didn't know what was involved.

Sarah was professional in her approach to the situation. She'd tried to acquire a budget because she realized that digital marketing was a "play to pay" environment (back in 2015) and "free" organic posts could no longer break through the clutter of posts on social media (Facebook, Instagram, etc.).

The real problem here wasn't Sarah - it was her environment and a leadership structure that didn't understand her or her team's need to be successful and to do what they were asked to do.

And Sarah's not alone. As I continue to work in digital

marketing, I see this phenomenon play out over and over again - even outside of marketing. It happened to me when I was working at a Fortune 500 company, as well as with smaller organizations.

Here's the pattern that I see.

1) Senior management, comprised mostly of Baby Boomers and olde Gen X'ers, recognizes that they need to "do" digital marketing.

2) But they don't know what "digital marketing" is at the present time (or, if they once knew, they haven't kept up with the latest developments).

3) They look at younger people as "knowing" what it is - either internally or as an outside agency - so they hire the agency or turn to their internal team and want them to "do digital marketing" for them.

4) Because senior management doesn't understand digital marketing, they aren't "leading the team" other than that: tasking them with doing effective digital marketing.

5) Without any understanding about what's involved with digital marketing, they don't know what's required for success or how to measure it.

I've been talking about marketing so far, but this plays out in other functions and industries, too.

For example, in retail and e-commerce, it's important to understand what's possible when it comes to technology, and what the latest platforms can do. I just got off a call with a friend who owns and runs a small candy store in New England. She was shut down by COVID-19 and has been asking customers to buy by phone - placing orders they can pick-up curbside.

This is how many restaurants and other food retailers have tried to weather the COVID-19 storm. Delivery and curbside options are their only way out and, if they've not enabled customers to order online, they're behind the curve. Now, my friend is thinking about easier ways for customer to place an online order. But her website won't accommodate that, so she's asking me for advice on how to do it quickly.

Do you know others who are facing the same technology challenges? Either in the aftermath of COVID-19 or for other reasons?

Think for a moment about other industries that have been challenged by "digital transformation." There are few that haven't!

For those among us who have struggled with the challenges and opportunities of technology, we may be facing a number of issues. At the logistical level, moving to a newer technological platform or model can be expensive. On top of that, everyone involved needs to learn the new technology and processes, which can involve training and getting started. And there's the added expense of moving to a new platform, software package, or system.

But we only get to the issues of logistics and cost once we've gone through an earlier process involving the decision-making. Before a new technology is approved and purchased, it has to be compared to others, priced out properly, and assessed versus its competition.

Going back in the process even further, an organization needs to learn about as many different competitors in the market as possible, to be sure they're making an informed decision. And these all need to be sampled, maybe even tested. This can take time and internal resources when it comes to the work and the research.

And taking it even one step further, backing up the process of switching to a new technology, there has to be a perception that there's a need to change. After all, there's so much work involved moving to a new technology (as we just described) that if there really isn't a problem to begin with – if the pain of not switching technologies or making a technological leap forward isn't big enough – then it's not even worth pursuing in the first place.

Taking a look back at this process: from seeing there's a problem or issue to be resolved all the way to researching alternative methods and technologies and purchasing, it's no wonder that many senior-level executives have passed along - or simply ignored - the work it takes to learn all the new digital marketing technologies.

Digital marketing is changing all the time; if you don't keep up with the new channels and platforms, tactics and techniques, it will pass you by quickly and feel insurmountable. This is where many leaders have given up and, while recognizing it's important, thrown it "over the proverbial wall" to the marketing function to figure it out and make recommendations, as well as run campaigns.
Just because it's hard, however, that doesn't mean it shouldn't be done. Especially if "keeping up" means staying relevant as the world marches inexorably forward in shifting technologies.

All of which is to say this: just because it's not easy to do, or even intimidating, it's no excuse for people not to try. And for many in senior level roles, I've noticed that they not only gave up trying, they don't feel that it's important for them to know about the details. After all, that's why they pay others (individual contributors, teams, and agencies) to do that work.

In Sarah's case, I'm happy to say that she came through this with flying colors. How was that possible, given where she was when we first met? We're going to review the way that happened, but to do that we need to take a quick detour into the world of science.

CHAPTER 5: THE SCIENCE REVELATION

How did Sarah get to a happy outcome? And how can other Millennials, like her, achieve happier outcomes at work? In fact, why can't everyone be happier at work? Does work satisfaction depend on the generation you're in?

The answer is no. It does not.

There are a number of assumptions to examine, so let's start with how people feel, or react, to situations based on their age category. We have been categorizing people into generational blocks because it makes life easy. This group does this, the other one does that, and that's just who they are. But are those assumptions and categorizations true?

Generalizations "by generation"

Here's one example: the myth that Baby Boomers didn't take the Coronavirus threat seriously. It started with this tweet from journalist Brigid Delaney on March 15, 2020: "In an unsettling reversal of my teenage years, I am now yelling at my parents for going out."

That tweet took off, with more than 34,000 retweets and thousands of people chiming in with sympathetic responses, as if she'd tapped into a phenomenon in the U.S. at that moment. From there, other publications repeated the idea, expounding on the idea and proposing reasons why Baby Boomers were ignoring or shrugging off the importance of the Coronavirus and COVID-19.

And in this way, a new urban myth was born, perpetuated because it told an interesting (counter-intuitive) story that was fundamentally false, as proven by a national poll by Morning Consult, which tracked public reactions to the virus since January.

The data indicates that 87% of Baby Boomers were "practicing social distancing measures," compared with 83% of Gen X'ers, 76% of Millennials, and 73% of Gen Z. These numbers indicate not only an acute awareness and an acceptance of importance, but also the reality that Boomers were being more cautious than any other age group!

There are many other assumptions about age groups. Here's an article from Inc. magazine called "4 Key Generational Trends in the Workplace." Do these trends resonate with you? Do you think they are accurate?

1. Baby Boomers are the most engaged and loyal generation.
2. Baby Boomers have the most faith in their organization's strategy.
3. Millennials find less meaning in their work.
4. Millennials are least satisfied with their pay.

I don't doubt that the data in this study created interesting findings, representing the group of people they interviewed. The fault lies in generalizing these findings across all organizations, for entire age groups.

Take, for example, the last point, that Millennials are the "least satisfied" about pay.

Is this true if you hold all other factors and differences (as variables) constant? (That's a nerdy data question.) I can tell you that for women, as another general group of which I am a member, we have been very disappointed with our pay - for a long time. I've been working for over two decades, for different organizations, and I can tell you that I've been extremely unsatisfied with my pay most of the time, especially as I've learned that I've been consistently under-paid versus my male counterparts.

So did they look at the Millennials being unsatisfied with their pay, as compared with other groups? Particularly women or other minority groups? There's a lot of data saying that non-white women experience the worst pay gaps. How does this compare with Millennials? It's when you think about all these other groups that the questions begin to arise about the process of categorizing itself.

Other generalizations – have you heard these?

Once you start paying attention to the various ways generalizations are made, the generalizations about age groups are everywhere. And while some of them may resonate as "true" with us, they need to be examined closely. Here are some more examples:

- Boomers are formal in their writing styles, whereas Millennials are casual.
- Boomers prefer the phone or email, while Millennials prefer chat or messaging.

How they differ at work	Millenials	Gen X'ers	Baby Bomers
Loyalty	Little to none	Loyal if opportunity for advancement	Most engaged and loyal
Engagement with work	Less engaged	Responsible and self motivated	Have faith in organizations
Social approach at work	Collaborative, seek feedback and guidance	Rugged individuals with good work ethic	Rugged individuals with good work ethic
View of authority	Respect must be earned, not demanded	Work around or influence authority, as needed	Pay your dues first, authority is earned
Use of technology	Expect tech, to make work more efficient, as often as possible	Comfortable with most technology	Not as comfortable with all new technologies
How they like to communicate	Prefer mobile messaging with colleagues	Value communication, not micro-management	Prefer email or verbal communication

https://managementisajourney.com/understanding-and-managing-the-4-generations-in-the-workplace/

Have you seen tables such as this, where more broad generalizations are made?

While there are often kernels of truth to some of these generalizations (which is how they became generalizations in the first place), the problem is that the second you pronounce them, there are "exceptions to the rule." But the allure of sweeping generalizations is that it makes the problem sound easy to pinpoint and, for many, easy to solve.

In fact, a small industry within HR has grown up around principles like these. Consider:
- Team building exercises
- Team building retreats
- Trust-building exercises
- HR modules for management

All of these are based on the assumptions that Millennials are a certain way, differing from Gen X'ers and Boomers because of "their generation" and the times during which they were raised. During the shelter-in-place stage of the Coronavirus, additional articles were being published about how Millennials were faring, including:

- Why the COVID-19 economy is particularly devastating to millennials, in 14 charts
- These workers feel less connected to their teams
- Millennials are getting stung by back-to-back economic crises
- Millennials are the new lost generation

While all these may be true, it's important to understand the flaw in the assumptions that Millennials are somehow "unique," as are Baby Boomers, as are Gen X'ers. The flaw in all the assumptions that writers and publications are making is the one thing that all the generations have in common: we're all human.

Why being human matters

It may seem obvious but the fact that we're all human matters because of the assumptions that are made - based on when someone was born or into what generation they fall. This is where the science comes in.

Let's start with the human brain.

Back in 1994, Antonio Damasio, a neuroscientist, stumbled upon an interesting fact about the decision-making part of the human brain. He studied various people who had damage in the part of the brain where emotions are generated. He found that these people seemed "normal" in every way, except that they didn't feel any emotions.

And they all had another trait in common: they couldn't make decisions.

This was novel and ground-breaking. Consider: whenever you make a decision based on "facts" - *you aren't really making that decision based on facts.* You're making a decision based on a "gut feeling," or you're leaning in one direction or another based on an emotion.

This makes sense when people talk about "just having a feeling" about something, and "going with their gut." What they sensed was the emotions they had swaying them in one direction versus another and they trusted what they were feeling. Even if it meant that they were going against what the "facts" were telling them.

This also explains why people of different backgrounds or political persuasions don't seem to be at all swayed by what their opponents, or others, refer to as "the facts;" instead, a person's decision-making process seems to be set, or highly influenced, by the emotions that the decision creates or fosters. This has huge implications in many areas and industries.

In 2010, an article in Psychology Today outlined the connection between emotion and logic, and how what one might refer to as "logical decisions" are predominantly molded by emotions. "Emotions have tremendous action potential. Yet the drive that emotions provide, particularly in the workplace, is sometimes experienced as stress related..."

Or, as the article's title says, "like it or not, emotions will drive the decisions you make today."

Primary Emotions

There's an interesting TED talk by scientist Natasha Sharma, who reveals how our emotions drive our daily decisions. She says we make approximately 35,000 decisions in one day. She then notes that people don't take care of their "emotional health" and "emotional fitness" the way they take care of their physical fitness, or mental fitness (doing crossword puzzles, for example). As youngsters, we're not taught how to deal with our emotions.

She says that people associate conventional wisdom with success and happiness in life. But people who show higher levels of "emotional fitness" are - in her studies and others - more likely to be happier and successful in later life.

Emotional fitness is going to be critical going forward, she says, because of the rate of change going on in the world right now. Our mental ability to deal with this rapid pace of change, and a faster, more automated world, has not changed, however, so we are not all as able to "keep up." And this means that people are becoming more stressed, and having more anxiety. So it will be more crucial than ever for people to be able to manage their emotions.

This is particularly true for younger people, who are dealing with many stressful situations in life. Consider: the average income for people age 18 - 35 has gone down for the past 25 years, while the cost-of-living has increased (Natasha gave this TED talk in 2017, so it was long before the Coronavirus stopped the world, and more young adults, age 22 – 25, found themselves unemployed than ever before).

She goes on to note that the majority of jobs being created are part-time or contract. Meanwhile, student debt is the highest it's ever been, and wealth disparity in the U.S. is the highest it's ever been.

Of all the emotions, she notes, there are only three that matter the most when it comes to driving our decision-making processes: love, hate and fear.

Natasha asserts that, at some point in our lives, we will feel as though "someone has wronged us" and they have to "pay for it."

Feelings of hate and anger keep us "stuck" on that idea, so it's important to let those emotions go. And the only way to eradicate those emotions is to change our expectation of the world as a "just and equal place" - because it's not.

Sometimes life is not fair; sometimes, people hurt us. This is part of the human experience, so if individuals can learn how to come to terms with these emotions, and reach the realization that 'life is not fair,' they will be able to let go of fear and hate.

The implications in the work environment are many: we're afraid of failure, we're afraid of not being acknowledged or appreciated, we're afraid of getting hurt, we're afraid of the unknown. We're afraid of many things, including losing our jobs/livelihood.

"Your emotions rule," she notes, "so learn to rule your emotions," she advises.

Implications in the workplace

Let's think about the implications this new information has on how we look at the workplace. In 2007, Wharton professor Sigal Barsade, an award-winning researcher/teacher who studies the influence of emotions in the workplace wrote, "Emotions travel from person to person like a virus."

"The state of the literature shows that affect matters because people are not isolated 'emotional islands.' Rather, they bring all of themselves to work, including their traits, moods and emotions, and their affective experiences and expressions influence others," according to the paper, co-authored by Donald Gibson of Fairfield University's Dolan School of Business.

She suggests that "while some people are better than others at controlling their emotions, that doesn't mean their coworkers aren't picking up on their moods. 'You may not think you are showing emotion, but there's a good chance you are in your facial expression or body language. Emotions we don't even realize we are feeling can influence our thoughts and behaviors."

People "bring all of themselves to work, including their traits, moods and emotions, and their… experiences and expressions influence others."

So it's important to consider what it means to have all these emotions playing out in the workforce, all day long.

If a worker believes that life should be fair, for example, and is fearful of losing her position, it can make her miserable. Layer that with other issues - she's not feeling "respected" at work by her colleagues, and she isn't getting the funding she needs, from her boss, for her team and their work - and it's understandable now why Sarah was so upset by the time I met with her. All that fear was creating a highly stressful situation for her.

Emotions are not acknowledged at work because it's a value-laden word

Looking at this research, it's clear that there are emotions playing out in the workplace - because we're all human. But there's an important contradiction: there's no place for emotions in the workplace.

"Emotion affects so many parts of work, from collaboration to decision-making, motivation, and communication between employees and managers. But in American culture, 'emotional' can be a dirty word. There's a misconception that expressing feelings is unprofessional or out of place in the office."

If you ask Baby Boomers and Gen X'ers, who are often the senior management and leaders in organizations, whether they're being emotional, perhaps sending emotional signals to others, they may deny it. Emotion has no place at work - only because they don't acknowledge that it's happening all around them, all the time, including amongst themselves. Yet everyone picks up on these signals, in body language or spoken words, consciously or unconsciously.

Each organization has its own culture. What's yours?

If you're not sure, you can get a sense from answering this question: what's a story that you can tell - about your organization - that would "only happen there?"

One example, from IDEO's New York studio, is that one day a week, their lunches are "dedicated to Make(believe) time." This allows employees to explore their creativity, even if it sounds silly or goofy. Other signals might be silly GIFs that circulate the office, or idiosyncratic messaging from senior management.

Why is the emotional culture important at work? Because when employees feel supported (and motivated) by their colleagues, they are happier and will stay in the organization longer - and they are probably more productive, too. Most importantly, it helps employees to deal with stresses better and to trust their colleagues and management more.

All this leads to a better working environment for everyone.

But emotions are there – even if they're not appreciated or acknowledged

What happens in the workplace if everyone is acting out of his/her own emotional intelligence and personal state, but it's not being acknowledged? And, in fact, people are told to keep their emotions out of their decision-making?

There's a perpetuation of the myth that everything that happens in the office is fact-based, merit-based, and fair. It's going the way it should be. When, in reality, it's not that way at all.

In reality, as Natasha Sharma noted, everyone is acting out of basic emotions: love, hate, and fear - with fear being the one that comes into play the most, in many work situations. Looking back at Sarah, she exhibited all of the worst reactions to her situation: she was fearful about losing the respect of her colleagues/teammates, fearful about not being able to do her job (without budget), and fearful about losing her position, based on what she perceived was an impossible situation.

The interesting part of this was how others around her felt about the same situation. Let's consider, for a moment, the emotional experience of her boss - the one who consistently denied her the budget she requested. Why would he do that? Why would he expect her to do her job well and, in her mind, deny her the means to achieve her goals?

Back to why being human matters

This is where science makes the work situation most interesting - specifically, understanding that everyone has emotions that are driving decision-making at work. Because Sarah's manager, and his bosses, are also dealing with their own emotions in their decision-making processes.

The beauty of understanding why and how humans work - how everyone acts and reacts in the work environment - is that the generalizations we make here apply universally. There are no exceptions to the rule, as happens so often with generalizations about age groups.

That said, we do need to take into account how individuals manage their emotions; that becomes unique and individual. But looking for and understanding the emotions in every person, at every level, is a great starting place for understanding what's going on – in teams, in organizations, and in outside vendors, etc.

I had the opportunity to meet with Sarah's boss, as well as other members of her senior management team. This gave me a great perspective on what was going on at the upper levels of management that affected Sarah's team. And the most interesting – though not surprising – finding was that Sarah's boss was acting out of fear, also.
What fears did he have? Here are just some of them:

- Fear of providing budget that was poorly spent
- Fear of not getting results he needed for his manager
- Fear and confusion, not understanding why Sarah kept coming to him for budget
- Frustration that Sarah's team didn't perform well
- Frustration with Sarah that she didn't understand that funding was given after she performed well
- Fearful for the stability of his own position, given the poor performance from Sarah's team
- Reluctance to speak with his boss about budget

      - because that conversation made him look bad
      when he, himself, couldn't justify the spend

As you can see, that's a lot of fear! It's no wonder that Sarah was being stonewalled every time she brought up the subject of budgets.

Bridging the gap

There was a huge chasm of communication, trust and understanding between Sarah's team and their management. And it was caused, primarily, by their lack of understanding when it came to digital marketing. This is why I have named this phenomenon the digital divide.

How does one bridge that gap? In Sarah's case, it involved meeting with everyone involved and educating them about the pieces they were missing. In this case, senior management needed to know enough about digital marketing to understand why budget was needed for the team to be successful. And for Sarah's team, it meant helping them to work in a new and different way, so that their efforts would be appreciated by senior management.

This involved teaching them about strategy, goals, and metrics.

While each case is different, in terms of the exact strategies and meetings, the goal is always the same: understanding that each generation - each individual - has her/his emotions at work.

Clarifying what those emotions are and what decision-making they drive is key. The best way to empower every generation in the workplace is to work with every individual, treating them as an individual, rather than dealing with classifications of age groups. This is a fundamentally - almost radically - different approach from others who teach how to resolve these issues in the workplace.

CHAPTER 6 – WHAT WE STAND TO LOSE

What do we stand to lose if we don't empower all the generations in the workplace? A lot. I look at and use data because it helps us to get outside of our personal, subjective views to see what's really going on.

Here's some interesting information that indicates we have a great deal to lose if we don't start to empower all the generations at work, so we work together more harmoniously.

Let's begin by viewing Millennials as an age group that's experienced a great deal of stress already in their lifetimes. As noted in The Atlantic in April 2020, in the midst of the coronavirus' "shelter in place" around the globe:

> *Millennials entered the workforce during the worst downturn since the Great Depression. Saddled with debt, unable to accumulate wealth,and stuck in low-benefit, dead-end jobs, they never gained the financial security that their parents, grandparents, or even older siblings enjoyed.They are now entering their peak earning years in the midst of an economic cataclysm more severe than the Great Recession, near guaranteeing that they will be the first generation in modern American history to end up poorer than their parents.*

In fact, research indicates that younger aged workers, entering the labor force during a recession (as in 2008 and the early recovery), as millions of Millennials did, creates early wage losses that take years to make up - if they are made up at all. The same will be true for Gen Z'ers entering the labor force in 2020.

Stung by these back-to-back economic crises, it's understandable that Millennials may feel that the cards have been stacked against them. Many graduated from college with unprecedented levels of student debt, only to enter the labor force with lower wages (due to the recession), which stayed relatively low over time, rather than growing, as they had done for the Baby Boomer generation and Gen X'ers.

In addition, when compared to other generations at the same point in their lives, Millennials have lower levels of home ownership, net worth, and real income, according to a 2018 Federal Reserve Board of Governor's paper. That means they're "behind everyone else" when it comes to their economic status in the labor force - and, in many ways, fighting for survival in this new recession/depression, or hanging on as best they can to their jobs.

When forced into telecommuting during the spring of 2020 and the coronavirus "shut in," Millennials (and Gen Z) also had the most difficulty adjusting to and working in the new work environment. For example, they reported a variety of work issues:

- 48% of Gen Z and 46% of Millennial workers described communicating with colleagues as "difficult," compared with 35% of Gen Xers and 36% of Baby Boomers.
- 50% of both Gen Z and Millennial workers said it was hard to get status updates from co-workers when everyone is working remotely, though only 40% of Gen Xers and 39% of Boomers felt the same way.
- 44% of Gen Z and 42% of Millennial workers said getting the information they've needed to work effectively has been difficult, as opposed to 33% of both Gen Xers and Boomers.

Understanding the economic framework for the Millennial generation, as well as where they come from in their frustrations with the "new normal' of work, here's what we stand to lose if we can't make the workplace better for them, as well as for all the other generations.

Workers will leave if they don't feel valued and unappreciated.

When I speak with people of all generations and ask where their workplace unhappiness stems from, many of them say the same thing: they don't feel appreciated.

Millennials grew up being rewarded for "showing up." It was common practice that "everybody gets a trophy for their effort." This made them feel as though they should always be rewarded for their efforts, not necessarily the outcome.
But this is not how business works. Most people are rewarded at work for results - as well as how well they get along with others - not how hard they work. This is a cruel reality and awakening for Millennials.

Baby Boomers often feel unappreciated for their wisdom and experience. They feel as though they've "been around the block" and offer value to the organization for what they know, what they've accomplished, and what they've seen or witnessed in their industry over time. Having this tossed aside, or undervalued, is not only bad for the people at work - it's bad for the organization.

What if Baby Boomers and Gen X'ers, who have 20 years of experience, can help an organization avoid a mistake - perhaps recalling something was tried a few years ago and failed? Does anyone remember the "New Coke" launch disaster? There's something to be said for the wisdom of history - so the same mistakes are not repeated.
When people feel valued and appreciated - no matter what their age or generation - they are often happier. And when people are happier, they're not only more likely to stay at their organization but also much more pleasant to be around!

Workers leave an organization, most often, because of their manager.

There's a saying that people don't leave because of the organization - they leave because of their manager. This holds true for any age group or generation.

Millennials sometimes feel as though their manager isn't listening to them, so they don't feel "heard." One example is their approach to tasks or activities that they know or believe "could be done better/faster if it were automated."

But when they make these suggestions, they are not usually empowered to make the process change and are told, instead, to do the task a certain way, perhaps how "it's always been done."

Managers or supervisors who are in an older age bracket may not have been trained on how to manage younger workers; so instead, they are doing what comes naturally, in some cases repeating how they, themselves were managed. Instead of receiving Millennial objections to "the way we do things here" as constructive and potentially innovative, they see it as revolting against them, against the norm, or pushback for no apparent reason.

If Gen X'ers and Baby Boomers aren't trained on the best management practices, they may make costly mistakes - losing good employees. Having to rehire costs the organization time and money; resources that don't have to be wasted if the best people are retained.

On the other side, for Gen X'ers and Baby Boomers who find themselves reporting to a Millennial manager, they can find it equally difficult.

Perhaps they're now reporting to someone younger because they were "passed over" for that role. Why? Once resentment starts, it's hard to deal with. Older employees hold a wealth of knowledge and experience, which should be appreciated and tapped; if an older employee is not ideal for a manager position, he/she should be helped to understand why and be given the chance to rectify it.

For this reason, older workers may feel unappreciated or "out of sync" with the younger team members, who may have their own language, habits, expressions, and ways of socializing that's foreign or different from their elder colleagues. So older workers may stop feeling "at home" or accepted on the team and, instead, feel excluded.

No one feels good when they're left out in the cold - this applies to adults as well as children!

Having older workers leave may be a way to cut costs for an organization, since older employees may be paid higher salaries because of tenure. But there's definitely age discrimination, and it should be addressed as carefully as every other type of illegal discrimination in the workplace.

There's a feeling that the "other generation" is a threat to job security and advancement.

Just because workers don't leave, it doesn't necessarily mean that all is well. The Olivet study also indicates that there could be resentment on both sides - from older and younger workers - that they are being "held back" at work, or their position is in jeopardy.
When asked "Do you feel a Boomer colleague is preventing you from advancing?" 30% of Millennials answered yes. That's one in three younger workers who feels that someone older is holding them back. No wonder there's resentment and, sometimes, passive aggressive or hostile communication from Millennials.

When Baby Boomers were asked "Are you worried that a Millennial could take your job?," 51% answered yes. That's half of all Boomers in organizations right now!

The research should have asked the exact same question of the Boomers, as this would have been a better comparison; however, this information still indicates that, potentially, half of all working Boomers are feeling insecure in their positions within their organizations.

Employees want to escape a "toxic work environment"

Perhaps the most disturbing data from the Olivet study is this: the survey asked each respondent if they plan to leave their job in the next six months and, if they said yes, it asked them why. 20% of the Millennials, who were planning to leave, wanted to "escape a toxic work environment." That's one-in-five of them. On the other hand, 27% of the Baby Boomers were planning to leave for the exact same reason; that's one-in-four.

What's creating these toxic work environments?

I look to leadership - managers at all levels - to create the work environment for everyone. If they can't create an atmosphere in which everyone can work, then they are failing as leaders. It's clear what we stand to lose if we don't change what's going on in many organizations. These toxic work environments are causing employees to be so unhappy that they will go elsewhere, if possible. Not to mention the disruption this must create when it comes to getting work done.

With all these emotions hanging in the air - resentment, fear, a "toxic" brew of culture and activities - it's no wonder that it sometimes feels like open warfare at work. And those of all generations who continue to work from home will not be able to avoid these emotions. As noted earlier, emotions come with us everywhere we go. So we need to develop our ability to see them, understand them, and understand what emotions others also may be feeling.

CHAPTER 7: REVELATIONS OF A MILLENNIAL IN HR

Jennifer L'Heureux is a Digital Leadership and Change Consultant, as well as a coach, facilitator and speaker, devoted to "elevating individuals and teams to become ready for tomorrow." Jennifer focuses on early and mid-career individuals, most often Millennials; she's a Millennial herself.

Because of her experience and her current role, I asked Jennifer if we could talk about her interest in inter-generational issues and her observations for this book. She agreed and I recorded our 20-minute conversation. If you'd like to see this in full, it's on my YouTube channel, or you can search for *Janet Granger Jennifer L'Heureux*. My questions, which I sent to Jennifer in advance, are in italics, as are my thoughts and comments as we spoke.

How did you become interested in the inter-generational issue?

I decided to go out on my own because I really love to help people, teams and organizations get ready for the future. Our lives are constantly changing – there's a saying that the rate of change we're experiencing right now is the slowest it's going to be in our lifetime, going forward. How do we get ready for that?

I thought about whom I wanted to work with and the Millennial generation stood out really strongly in my mind for a couple of reasons. I always say that I'm "on the cusp" of the Gen X'ers and the Millennials, but that's my generation. They're the people that are going to be the future. They're about 50% of the workforce right now... they have a "bad rap" -

but I don't believe it's warranted. I think it's the stereotype mentality - and a few can ruin it for many.

When I thought about who I wanted to work with, I thought "What's the energy I enjoy?" I enjoy that innovative, creative, "let's do anything," "anything is possible" energy; I wanted to work with this generation. I've also decided I don't want to use the term Millennial anymore, because it has such a negative connotation; I want to work with early to mid-career professionals, which is a large part of this generation.

I did some research on Millennials to learn: Where are the struggles? Where do we need to focus? And it wasn't just about Millennials or this group of professionals - it's about everyone. You can't look at things in a silo. You have to look at the big picture.

The big picture is the four generations we have in the workforce right now.

We have the Baby Boomers still there, we have the Gen X'ers, who I've learned sometimes feel a bit forgotten, we have the Millennials or Echo Boomers or Gen Y, and then you have this new generation – I've heard "I" Generation, Generation Z (Zed), the youngest group we have in the organization.

It's not just about that one generation. It's about everyone working together so we can develop our future leaders. If we want companies to survive – if we want our economy to survive – this is the group of people we have to make sure is ready for that.

Yes, in the U.S. they do comprise well over 50% of the workforce. And I agree with you that they have a "bad rap." Sure, there are bad apples in every generation. But, in some ways, I feel they are the misunderstood generation.

Given this, what has surprised you most, now that you've focused in on early to mid-career professionals?

The thing that has surprised me is how much people want this group to succeed! And I think they need this group to succeed. If we don't have over 50% of our workforce able to have the right mindset and critical thinking abilities, to make companies successful, everything's going to die out, or the Boomers are never going to be able to retire, if we look at it from that generation's perspective.

How do we get them (Millennials) to understand that basic foundation of business? To make sure that they are ready to run the professional world, but also not lose that innovation, that creativity, that curiosity, that belief that "we can do anything."
"We can do anything" has the caveat that we have the right foundation to build on.

The biggest thing I'm looking at is – and I don't think it was a surprise - I don't think anything that I've learned is a surprise (especially coming from this generation) - is just how much work needs to be done. Sometimes things aren't 'sexy,' but in order for you to get to that 'sexy' part of work, you need to do the things that are not 'sexy.'

The biggest surprise was that really nothing surprised me. Also, the passion, when I talk to people about this generation. There were no mediocre thoughts, or balanced thoughts; it was all passion - all strong opinions on this generation. There was no "well, they're alright." It was all, "Oh, let me talk to you about Millennials!"

And the Millennials I talked to said, "Oh, let me talk to you about my leaders!" There was no evenness to the conversation.

That's a great point. That's the point in this book, which is to approach everybody. You can't deal with one generation in a silo.

This science-based approach, which does look at emotions, and the huge role that emotions play in all of this, which is exactly the same thing as the passion you describe. We've come at it from two different points but arrived at exactly the same point, which is really interesting.

I think your point about wanting this group to succeed - coming at this from the marketing perspective, as opposed to the Human Resource perspective as you have - where I found that Millennials were struggling the most was that no one ever shared with them what "strategy" was.

And because they are the "we can do it" generation, they were finding all sorts of new and cool ways (to market), but weren't necessarily being told how they were going to be judged, in the end. What are the metrics of success? And that all their efforts should be focused on achieving those metrics of success.

It's imperative to realize that - in marketing - you can have a video go viral but - if you don't sell more widget -, we don't care. Millennials need to be told how they're going to be judged. What does success look like? Let's strategically work towards that.

I agree with that completely. And then - from the (Millennial) generation's perspective - is how we used to judge success the right way to do that now? Or does that also need to change, based on this new way of working that's coming? Because it's not just about the new generations in the workforce, it's how we work that is changing.

It's the gig economy. It's the flexible work arrangements. It's more contract-based and freelance work. Everything about how we work is changing, so how companies measure success, especially when it comes to the performance of their employees. Are we doing it the right way? - is the question. And that's why everyone needs to be at the table when we have these conversations.

Yes, that's so true. And are we accomplishing anywhere

near what we could accomplish if everyone was working well together. That leads me to my next question.

Is there anything you'd like to share with Boomers and Gen X'ers about what they really do need to know about Millennials? Using examples like being the innovators, and the "can do's" and "we can do it better." Or one of the great fallacies is…?

I've been thinking about these questions, since you sent them ahead of time, and they've been in the back of my head for a few days.
I sent them to you in advance so you'd have time to think about them.

And I think that's another thing that's different about the generations, that I don't think I needed my answers to be perfect, I didn't need to have 'the right answer,' I just needed to have that ability to think.

I think Millennials do like a lot of attention, but you can't see that as a bad thing. It means that they're really open to feedback. They want mentorship; they want to grow; they want to get better. So I don't want to come to you with the perfect solution because I want to think with you about what the perfect solution can be.

The conversation we're having right now is more meaningful to me than me, answering your questions.

I think that's a really good point. The whole collaborative approach is very Millennial. When I think back about my experience with the Boomer generation - and even the generation before me, the Greatest Generation - I would say they were not really collaborative.

And we're very team oriented.

And I love that team approach which is, "I don't have to be the smartest person in the room. Maybe if we bang it around all five of us will come up with an idea. I love that approach to problem-solving because then it doesn't all fall on me. It's something that the genius of the group can figure out.

I think it comes from that fact that we came from a generation that everyone got a medal.

Yes, it was a team effort.

Yes, it was a team effort, which, in a lot of ways, maybe caused some of the "issues" that are happening today. But how can we see those as strengths? How can we see that as we have this group, this generation, that doesn't have to be the peacock? That doesn't have to be the attention-seeking person in the room. I mean, there are these people in this generation who want to be the peacock. But in every generation there are those who want to be the peacock.

Yet, in general, they're much more open to feedback. They're much more open to insight. They want to work on a team. They want to work together; they want to be collaborative. So, how do we use that - to everyone's benefit? And how do you get to be part of their team?

It doesn't have to be a team of early to mid-career professionals, Millennials, or Gen Z. How do we make teams that are diverse - because there's strength in that - that's what we're talking about here. That it's not about one generation – it's about all the generations working together.

Yes, and success comes from harnessing every type of diversity that you can imagine: age diversity, cultural diversity, gender diversity. I think it's important to have all the voices at the table.

Yes, as a side story I was watching an interview with comedienne Tina Fey, and she said when they started letting female writers into the SNL Writer's Room, sketches that weren't put on the table before - because no one laughed at them in the writing room - got attention because you had another group of people laughing at them. And they went over very well with their audience which was 50% female!

We see things differently so having that different perspective, and being open to that different perspective, is important.

It's like you said, it's great if you have a thousand views, but what if you don't sell any widgets? It's one thing to be open to a different perspective; it's another to let it in. And let it be part of your overall strategy.

So the last question is, from the perspective of early to mid-career professionals, what do WE look like? What do older managers and decision-makers and owners and senior executives look like?

The reason I ask this question is that I found it most illuminating, talking to a Gen Z Influencer. To hear her perspective of older people made me think, "Oh! We look like THAT?" So I turned it 90 degrees to say, "If we LOOK like this, maybe it's because of this (fact)."

This was the toughest question that you gave me, for me to answer, because when I was thinking about it I thought, "Who are the Boomers that I know?" And the first ones that came to mind are my parents! My parents are Boomers. And I think all of our [Millennial's] parents are Boomers.

These are the people who raised us! These people who are running companies raised us, so our entire lives have been a relationship with this generation. I think a lot of how you see them will depend on the relationship you have with your parents.

And how good that interaction was.

Yes! My dad hated calling in sick to work. He thought it was the worst thing in the world. So now, I can't do that because I don't want to disappoint him. If you look at it that way, ultimately, especially if you have a really positive relationship with the people who raised you, you want to be what they want you to be.

You want to please them

Yes, you want to please them. Well, it's really that you don't want to disappoint them. It's more that. When you look at the older generation, it's really interesting.

So, looking back, do you think that the older generation was too devoted to work? Perhaps to their detriment? They haven't focused on themselves or their personal lives - it's all been "for work?"

100%! Right now, who doesn't know somebody who goes to a therapist? It's a new thing. That's not something my parents' generation did.

> "We didn't go talk to people about our problems. We went to work, Jennifer. We went and we got the job done. We didn't look at the underlying issues that were causing the stress, or the emotion. We didn't have emotions. We went to work. We made money for our family - we took care of our family."

I think that's where it comes from. When I look at the older generation, I'm really lucky that I've had some leaders in that generation who have been really open and more empathetic. And then I've had some that are just: "you do your job."

Put your head down. Do your work. Don't ask questions.

Don't ask questions. But if I'm not asking questions, how can we ever know if there's a better way to do it? Because the biggest thing I think we have to remember is, as much as our workforce is changing, our customers are changing, too.

And processes could change.

Processes could change. How we need to serve them (our customers). There's so much that can change - and if we just 'stick our head down, and do our job,' how are we ever going to get better?

I want to end on a thought which is – FYI, us Boomers were just like you when we were young.

Oh, I know!

When we entered the workforce, we had the same ideas, the same energy, the perspective of "Oh, there's a better way to do this - and I can tell you." And I think the frustration we met with, we're now turning around and imposing on the next generation. We came in wanting to change the world and ended up being copy-monkeys instead. And that's not going to work anymore.

For me, I go back to "How did I feel when I was met that way?" And a lot hasn't changed. What has changed is: How do you harness that (energy) now? As opposed to beating it down with Tthat's how we do things here." Which made me crazy when I was young.

Yes. I think the other thing is, some people are fine with being the "copy monkey," as you said, but tell me why the copies are important. Tell me how this fits into the bigger picture. Tell me how doing this is going to help me understand.

It's about systems thinking. We're part of a system. We're not one person. And it's all about the team but it's also a little bit about the individual, too, because teams are made up of individuals.

The other thing - if I'm putting it back on what Boomers need to realize - is that yes, you had the same troubles we did, but a "go to market strategy" was years in the past. It's so fast right now. How can you afford to take the time to push people down? What is the benefit of not finding the best idea?

Things are moving so much faster. How can we make sure that the best ideas are at the table? You and I, Janet, could have the best idea - but together, it's going to be a better idea.

How do we find the better idea?

Absolutely. And I think that, ultimately, for my generation, the hardest thing to accept is that the way we did it isn't going to work anymore. It's just not the best way. It was how we did it. But, to your point, the world is changing infinitely faster than it was. And, if you keep doing it "that way," you're going to end up a dinosaur, in the dust. I think that's very scary to a lot of people.

Yes, and I think it's going to be very interesting because, in five years, we're all going to have to remember how different it was five years ago! We're not going to be able to look back 20 years this time and say, it was so different 20 years ago. We're probably going to have five to seven years to get into a groove.

And then Gen Z is here!

Yes, and then they're going to be knocking on *our* doors.

The more we can work together, now, the easier it will be when we have to let in a new way of working as we get older, as time goes by, and as we get to a new generation.

This has been great. I appreciate your taking the time to share this with me. Any last thoughts?

Well, I could go on and on. But I think the biggest thing I want to say to everyone is, the only way we're going to get through this together is to keep this conversation going. Let's have more of these conversations. Let's talk about "How do we develop our future leaders?"

How do we modernize – though I don't like the term modernize – but how do we modernize our Boomers in the world? How do we do that so we can meet in a place that's going to create a stronger bond, and a stronger company, and more impact for the world around us?

CHAPTER 8: REVELATIONS OF A GEN Z INFLUENCER

In my research for this book, I stumbled across an interesting video by YouTube Influencer Jordan Theresa, a 21 year-old British citizen who has grown her following doing make-up tip videos. She has branched out her topics into social commentary, speaking to and for her generation (Gen Z) and, at this writing, she has over 92,000 subscribers to her channel; her most recent video has over 229,000 views.

I found her video on Youth Bashing, as she calls it, because it is titled: "Ok, boomer - the war between millennials and baby boomers." I was hooked at the title.

While Jordan is a Gen Z herself, she did extensive research on the different generations, starting with Baby Boomers and moving through Gen X, Millennials, and her generation, Gen Z.

I was particularly impressed by the depth and breadth of her research, which she shared during the first part of the video, going into the history of youth bashing, which she noted has been a favorite past-time since the ancient Greeks and noting that, because of its longevity, it was most likely here to stay - at least for the moment.

From there, she went on to talk about the phenomenon from her generation's perspective; her revelations were insightful.

I reached out to Jordan to see if she would be up for an interview for this book. Since the goal of this video was to "start a conversation," as she explained, she appreciated my reaching out to her and graciously agreed. This chapter is a summary of this conversation and has been reviewed and approved by her, to be sure that the message I send out is accurate and fair.

How did you get the idea to do the "youth bashing" video?

Jordan: I noticed that in one of the newspapers here, the Daily Mail - a commentator - wrote that the phrase "Ok, Boomer" is like the "n" word of ageism. I was appalled at the comparison! There's no way that the phrase "ok, Boomer" is as offensive. It seems like all the Boomers are able to do this youth bashing of Millennials, I see it all the time. But the moment someone younger says something back, they're all upset. There's a clear double-standard when it comes to nicknames and phrases like that. And there's no way that there's a comparison to the "n" word at all.

It's clear you did a lot of research before you did the "youth bashing" video. Did anything surprise you that you learned?

It was enormously helpful to do all that research ahead of time. I spend about five days researching the pieces that I do; I don't know if people realize the time I put in. I found a lot of resources - that's how I found the quote from the Daily Mail that I was just talking about, and others in The Sun. Wikipedia ended up being the most helpful, actually.

When I was researching the U.S., I learned about Ronald Reagan. I had no idea who he was and his theories and what he did, when it comes to economics, really did surprise me. Boomers were the largest voting group and the conservatism at the time helped vote him in. His actions in office contributed to the increase of income inequality in the U.S. One statistic is between 1979 and 2007, the top 1% of American earners saw a 278% income increase, while those American Earners in the top 40 – 60% only saw a 35% increase.

This blew my mind, also: since 1980, college costs have

increased 600%, and that's adjusted to inflation.

Thinking now about the Boomer and Gen X'ers who are reading this, what would you like to share about Gen Z that they should know?

Well, we can start with the negatives to be first. Millennials say that Gen Z is "inappropriate" and that's a fair statement, in many cases. My generation has been so fixated on their phones and social media that we don't necessarily know how to read people. We don't know how to "read a room," as they say. So we're not thinking about how something that we say may be heard or interpreted.

That's something we need to do better. We need to address the fact that we don't read people well and we need to learn how to do that better. I think a lot of the criticism about us being inappropriate is because we don't think about how our comments will be received. And we don't want to be hurtful. It just comes out that way sometimes.

The other comment is that our generation is selfish: it's all me, me, me. I believe that's true, to some extent. And that needs to change.

On a positive note, Gen Z are very empathetic and care a lot. At least the women I know. I can't speak for the men; I've noticed that some men or boys are less empathetic about people with a different upbringing. There are still homophobic, racist, and misogynistic people and three Twitter accounts that are horrible in that area.
My generation cares about the world and other people – such as the disabled - and we want to make a difference. The minute we start to talk about politics and our values, though, we get shut down. At least publicly.

I associate with like-minded people though – I think we all do, even a bit too much. That's why I wanted to start this conversation, to hear from others.

Just because I care - we care - doesn't mean we're pushovers. We know our rights here, in the U.K. and we'll stand up for them. We push back and we're not shy about it.

How or why did you start doing YouTube videos?

I've had jobs working at companies. I hated it. Our generation has a hatred of capitalism, and taking advantage of everyday workers. We're very entrepreneurial, and a great example of this is YouTube. There are so many YouTube channels; people, like me, doing videos on clothing, fashion, you name it.

I do beautician work, too. But I prefer working for myself. Most of our generation wants to work for themselves. We're all aware of what we get paid, for an hourly wage, and what our companies make based on our labor. That's sheer exploitation.

Take Jeff Bezos and Amazon. It's a shady company to work for. They abuse their workers and the working-class. But I still buy from them.

Tell me more about that. If you believe Amazon exploits its employees, why do you buy from them? Isn't that contradictory?

Yes, but it turns into a class issue. I'm from the working-class and the working-class, like me, buy what they can afford. They need to buy things that are cheap because of what they make.

And then yes, as you say, they are the most affected by what Amazon does. Until they can afford to spend their money more ethically, they are stuck with buying what they can afford. It's a vicious cycle.

I shared with Jordan what I appreciated, in her video, in her observations about Baby Boomers. And then I shared my experience with her, to give her more background than she would find in resources like Wikipedia. I shared that when we were younger - her age - many of us were also politically active, protesting against what we saw as the causes of injustice in our world, like apartheid in South Africa. Many of us considered ourselves rebels - in our own way. We may now be "the establishment" to push back against but we view ourselves differently, at least in our past.

Perhaps this is the reality (and curse?) of every generation as it ages: to be rebellious in youth and then be considered part of the problem as we age. There are rebels from our generation, from every generation, still hard at work fighting inequality and discrimination.

Jordan was interested to hear my take on this and our conversation ended with us learning from one another - perhaps the best way to move forward towards better communication and understanding between and among the various generations.

CHAPTER 9: REVELATIONS ON MAKING IT WORK

Now that we have a sense of what's at stake, we need to help organizations resolve the current enmity in the workplace. So let's talk about how to make the situation better. Our goal should be creating a pleasant and amiable work environment - rather than one that's "toxic" - and a place where employees want to stay (at least for a while), rather than leave.

This idea isn't new. In fact, there are many Human Resource strategies and techniques that have arisen to address this issue. Let's look at a few to see why these haven't worked so far.

Onboarding Materials

Think, for a moment, about a new hire. How do they feel in the first day of work? If you can't remember your first day, here are some ideas to consider:

First, they accepted the job offer, so something resonated in the description of what they were going to do or the manager they will report to - and perhaps met in the interviewing process.

Second, they want to stay at the organization; after all, they wouldn't have committed to it if they didn't think it would suit their goals, at least for a while.

And third, they're a bit scared and expectant and, most likely, nervous. They're about to be plunged into an environment where they'll spend most of their waking hours, five days a week, and they typically don't have any idea who their colleagues will be or what that experience will be like.

Now that you're into the mindset of a new hire: What type of onboarding materials will prepare you for the experience of working with people from different walks of life, at different ages and stages in their careers? And with all the other onboarding materials, including benefits decisions and (possibly) handbook materials: What will have an impact and help you, as an employee, to deal with someone who's old enough to be your parent, or young enough to be your child?

While onboarding materials can be helpful, when it comes to setting up expectations about the culture of an organization, they aren't close to a "real life" experience. Even showing a video about the organization is still a passive experience. There's nothing more educational than being part of an experience; "materials" presented before an employee even enters the organizations culture can only go so far.

HR Modules and Slides

If you're an employee experiencing difficult issues at work, which can range from the stress of your role and getting work done, what impact will an HR module, or a meeting where you sit and listen to your manager go through a slide presentation, have on how you feel?

Believe it or not, these types of modules and presentation decks are available online, for sale, with the promise of addressing a range of issues, including this generation gap in the workplace.

How many times have you sat through a presentation, as interesting as it was at the time, only to have it become a distant memory a few days later? The presentation of slides, or an HR module designed for use by anyone and everyone, doesn't carry anywhere near the weight of something that's a real-life experience, with longevity.

Team Meetings, Team-building Exercises, and Retreats

Real-life experiences, like team meetings, exercises and retreats, take this learning more seriously and can create impact for both employees and employers.

Experiences like these are valuable because they help address emotions that people are feeling. They can create positive emotions which, in the company of people from work, can help create a positive view of team members and management. These are all good experiences to foster. The more intense the experience, the more people can get out of it.
The only problem with team meetings, exercises and retreats isn't what happens during the experience; the issue is what happens afterwards.

Coming "back to the reality of the workplace" is where these experiences fall down. Speaking personally, going from an event or a day outside the workplace, where people have a good time, or work together on a meaningful task (such as helping a neighborhood, or a community), only to fall back into old habits and realities back at work is a real let-down.

Yes, the meeting or experience was enjoyable at the time, but its effects don't last very long. Friendships may have formed and better conversations may have taken place, but there's always the issue of going back to the place where the issues began and changing what's there, too.

Plus, there may be bad feelings (such as fear) that haven't been addressed, which continue to lurk beneath the surface of work interactions. That's the fallback of using these approaches.

Management Training

Not everyone is prepared to manage people. In fact, the typical pattern in an organization is to take someone who is very good at their job, remove them from doing the work that they're good at and, suddenly, make them responsible for managing other people, doing that same type of work.

Often, this promotion and great opportunity is presented without any training, leaving the individual to figure out for him/herself how to transition from one type of work to the other.

What is a person to do when thrust into this new role? Often, they will repeat the patterns they are used to; that is, they will manage other people the same way they have been managed, since that's what they know.

In the best case, they've been managed by someone who is good or great in this role. In the worst case, they are repeating bad patterns of behavior. Since many people leave organizations because of bad supervisors or managers, this can have severely detrimental consequences in losing good and talented people.

So what works?
The good news is that there are ways to make this transition work - if not perfectly, all the time, then better, for all involved!

In my experience, working with all generations, what works best is:

- Uncovering the fears of each person
- Understanding what everyone has at stake
- Revelations and sharing in a safe environment (without judgement or recrimination)
- Mentoring for all age groups (including reverse mentoring)

- Constant review and feedback

As you can see, this is not a quick bandage fix. It takes an intensive learning session, the patience to speak to everyone involved, an "outsider's perspective" on the inter-personal dynamics at work, and a commitment of everyone to make a change, creating daily and weekly habits that reinforce that change.

This moves us to the last chapter in this book - how to begin.

CHAPTER 10: HOW TO BEGIN TO RESOLVE THE INTERGENERATIONAL DIVIDE

This is where the rubber hits the road, as they say. Knowing everything about brain science now and how critical team cohesion is to an organization's success, as well what hasn't been working, where does one start?

I've always been most successful when I know what question to ask at the beginning… and the question for you is this: Do we have this problem in my organization? And, if the answer is yes - How bad is it?

That's the question: How bad is it? How do you know this is enough of a problem to act now?

The "Touching Base" Survey

The best way to answer this is by conducting a quick five-question survey to the team or organization in question. I've created a survey that does this in Survey Monkey and, once the comprehensive results are tabulated, you can see where you stand.

What are the questions in the survey?

It starts with a simple question about whether or not they are happy. This is a great way to open, showing that we want to know how they feel about where they are right now.

The questions continue with the same type of inquiry to understand their feelings about where they are in the organization. Because, as we noted earlier, what they feel will drive all their decision-making when it comes to how they interact with others and whether or not they will even stay with the organization.

Even if you're not sure that you want to move forward right now, the advantage of sending out this type of survey is to show your employees that you do care about how they feel about where they are in the organization and if they feel valued. It will open up the conversation and will show that there's a willingness to understand if there are underlying issues.

I'm a Millennial or Gen Z – Help!

Yes, I understand. In fact, the first person to ask me for help with this issue in the workplace was a Millennial! You're not the one in charge, necessarily; instead, you're a worker bee who's got their head down, doing the work, and feeling unappreciated and misunderstood. Believe me, I know many people like you!

Please feel free to reach out to me by email (yes, good old-fashioned email! I am a Baby Boomer, remember?): janet at janetgranger.com.

We'll set up a time to talk about your situation, and I can help you navigate the territory of communicating with your boss(es). In some cases, I'll send you the survey link so you can share it with your boss(es) and ask them to send it out to your team, so they can get a better understanding of what's truly going on beneath the surface. This is in their best interest, in order to get the team working effectively.

The Funding Question

For some of you, the question is a bit more practical: How do I get funding (or what funding do I use) to deal with any issues I may find, if I send out this survey?

In larger organizations, and enterprise companies, this funding typically comes from the area of "Diversity and Inclusion."

One of the best ways to establish that there is, in fact, a problem to be solved, is to show data. This quick survey is designed to do just that: taking the pulse of your employees and creating data to show whether or not there is a problem to be resolved. And the way it's designed is to have exactly what the problem is bubble up in the answers.

What to do if there's no funding

Please feel free to reach out to me via email at janet at janetgranger.com to talk about sending this quick survey out to your team or organization to get a sense of where they stand. Even if it's just to see where you are at the moment; this type of information can be extremely valuable as you plan your strategy going forward and as you work towards retaining your talented workers.

How do you know if there's tension brewing among Baby Boomers, Gen X'ers, Millennials, or the new Gen Z's you've hired? You may be seeing some of the signs I pointed out earlier: lack of conversation, rudeness, lack of engagement. This survey is a great way to have the answers you need - right at your fingertips. And it's easy to do – it takes only two minutes to fill out.

If you're still unsure, I am very approachable - please reach out to me by email: janet at janetgranger.com. I look forward to speaking with you about your particular situation.

REFERENCES AND LINKS

CHAPTER 1

Page 4 -The Rising Speed of Technological Adoption
https://www.visualcapitalist.com/rising-speed-technological-adoption/

CHAPTER 2

Page 10 – Generations in the Workplace Baby

Boomers https://www.tirebusiness.com/article/20150825/ NEWS/150829965/generations-in-the-workplace-baby-boomer

The Secret to Teamwork Across Generations https:// www.ccl.org/articles/leading-effectively-articles/the-secret-to-working-with-millennials/

Page 11 – Employer Branding and Onboarding: Keys to Recruiting and Retaining Top Millennial Talent in Power Generation https://www.powermag.com/employer-branding-and-onboarding-keys-to-recruiting-and-retaining-top-millennial-talent-in-power-generation/

The Secret to Teamwork Across Generations https:// www.ccl.org/articles/leading-effectively-articles/the-secret-to-working-with-millennials/

Page 12 – Getting Different Generations to Effectively Collaborate With One Another https://www. ngenperformance.com/blog/leadership-2/getting-different-generations-to-effectively-collaborate-with-one-another

Switch on what is best in every single person https://www.gallup.com/learning/

Why do 28% of employees quit in their first 90 days? Poor onboarding practices https://www.hrdive.com/news/why-do-28-of-employees-quit-in-their-first-90-days-poor-onboarding-practi/441139/

Study reveals relationship between millennials and Baby Boomers in the workplace https://online.olivet.edu/news/study-boomers-millennials-working-together

CHAPTER 3

Page 14 – What Is Team Building? You Can Use Team Building to Turn a Group of Individuals Into a Team https://www.thebalancecareers.com/what-is-team-building-1918270

Getting Different Generations to Effectively Collaborate With One Another https://www.ngenperformance.com/blog/leadership-2/getting-different-generations-to-effectively-collaborate-with-one-another

Why Diverse Teams Are Smarter https://hbr.org/2016/11/why-diverse-teams-are-smarter

Why diversity matters https://www.mckinsey.com/business-functions/organization/our-insights/why-diversity-matters

Page 16 – TMNT - Say No To Drugs Advert https://www.youtube.com/watch?v=s2kKjpNWHks&feature=player_embedded

CK "banned" ad https://www.youtube.com/watch?v=vZVk21Pco-c&feature=player_embedded

Study Reveals Relationship Between Millennials and Baby Boomers in the Workplace https://online.olivet.edu/news/study-boomers-millennials-working-together

A shocking 30% of Millennials feel that Boomers are holding them back in the workplace – Here's why. https://www.theladders.com/career-advice/millennials-baby-boomers-in-workplace

CHAPTER 5

Page 21- Baby Boomers Were Blasé About the

Coronavirus? Why Did We Believe That? https://www.nytimes.com/2020/04/29/opinion/sunday/coronavirus-baby-boomers.html

Coronavirus Content - https://morningconsult.com/wp-content/uploads/2020/04/2003128_crosstabs_CORONAVIRUS_CONTENT_Adults_v4_JB.pdf

4 Key Generational Trends in the Workplace- https://www.inc.com/dave-kerpen/4-key-generational-trends-in-workplace.html

Page 22 – Understanding and Managing the 4 Generations in the Workplace https://managementisajourney.com/understanding-and-managing-the-4-generations-in-the-workplace/

Page 23 – Why the Covid-19 economy is particularly devastating to millennials, in 14 charts https://www.vox.com/2020/5/5/21222759/covid-19-recession-millennials-coronavirus-economic-impact-charts

These workers feel 'less connected' with their teams https://www.hcamag.com/us/specialization/employee-engagement/these-workers-feel-less-connected-with-their-teams/221261

Millennials Are Getting Stung by Back-to-Back Global Crises https://www.bloomberg.com/amp/news/articles/2020-04-08/millennials-are-getting-stung-by-back-to-back-economic-crises

Millennials Don't Stand a Chance They're facing a second once-in-a-lifetime downturn at a crucial moment. https://www.theatlantic.com/ideas/archive/2020/04/millennials-are-new-lost-generation/609832/

Decisions are largely emotional, not logical https://bigthink.com/experts-corner/decisions-are-emotional-not-logical-the-neuroscience-behind-decision-making

Page 24 – Why What We Feel Matters More Than What We Think https://www.youtube.com/watch?v=DsDVCQnqcy4

Managing Emotions in the Workplace: Do Positive and Negative Attitudes Drive Performance? https://knowledge.wharton.upenn.edu/article/managing-emotions-in-the-workplace-do-positive-and-negative-attitudes-drive-performance/

Page 25 – Managing Emotions in the Workplace: Do Positive and Negative Attitudes Drive Performance https://knowledge.wharton.upenn.edu/article/managing-emotions-in-the-workplace-do-positive-and-negative-attitudes-drive-performance/

Turns Out Emotions Do Belong in the Workplace—Here's Why https://www.ideo.com/blog/turns-out-emotions-do-belong-in-the-workplace-heres-why

CHAPTER 6

Page 28 - Millennials Don't Stand a Chance They're facing a second once-in-a-lifetime downturn at a crucial moment. https://www.theatlantic.com/ideas/archive/2020/04/millennials-are-new-lost-generation/609832/

The Career Effects Of Graduating In A Recession https://www.nber.org/digest/nov06/w12159.html

Millennials Are Getting Stung by Back-to-Back Global Crises https://www.bloomberg.com/amp/news/articles/2020-04-08/millennials-are-getting-stung-by-back-to-back-economic-crises

Are Millennials Different? https://www.federalreserve.gov/econres/feds/files/2018080pap.pdf?utm_source=mandiner&utm_medium=link&utm_campaign=mandiner_202002

Younger Workers Having the Most Difficulty Working From Home https://finance.yahoo.com/news/younger-workers-having-most-difficulty-180641171.html

Page 30 – Study reveals relationship between Millennials and Baby Boomers in the workplace https://online.olivet.edu/news/study-boomers-millennials-working-together

CHAPTER 7

My interview with Jennifer L'Heureux: https://www.youtube.com/channel/UCQ9c6_CAYEeXvioe9KrpL1g

CHAPTER 8

Page 32 - Jordan Theresa https://www.youtube.com/user/snapbacksnstarbucks

Social Commentary https://www.youtube.com/playlist?list=PL1WjUC_7tmjeF9G5vzMggfDOwl7eCorAA

ok, boomer - the war between millennials & baby boomers https://www.youtube.com/watch?v=HCbE6tyRpXw&list=PLWjUC_7tmjeF9G5vzMggfDOwl7eCorAA&index=3&t=0s

9 781628 220087